Reforming U.S. Drone Strike Policies

COUNCIL *on*
FOREIGN
RELATIONS

Center for Preventive Action

Council Special Report No. 65
January 2013

Micah Zenko

Reforming U.S. Drone Strike Policies

The Council on Foreign Relations (CFR) is an independent, nonpartisan membership organization, think tank, and publisher dedicated to being a resource for its members, government officials, business executives, journalists, educators and students, civic and religious leaders, and other interested citizens in order to help them better understand the world and the foreign policy choices facing the United States and other countries. Founded in 1921, CFR carries out its mission by maintaining a diverse membership, with special programs to promote interest and develop expertise in the next generation of foreign policy leaders; convening meetings at its headquarters in New York and in Washington, DC, and other cities where senior government officials, members of Congress, global leaders, and prominent thinkers come together with CFR members to discuss and debate major international issues; supporting a Studies Program that fosters independent research, enabling CFR scholars to produce articles, reports, and books and hold roundtables that analyze foreign policy issues and make concrete policy recommendations; publishing *Foreign Affairs*, the preeminent journal on international affairs and U.S. foreign policy; sponsoring Independent Task Forces that produce reports with both findings and policy prescriptions on the most important foreign policy topics; and providing up-to-date information and analysis about world events and American foreign policy on its website, CFR.org.

The Council on Foreign Relations takes no institutional positions on policy issues and has no affiliation with the U.S. government. All views expressed in its publications and on its website are the sole responsibility of the author or authors.

Council Special Reports (CSRs) are concise policy briefs, produced to provide a rapid response to a developing crisis or contribute to the public's understanding of current policy dilemmas. CSRs are written by individual authors—who may be CFR fellows or acknowledged experts from outside the institution—in consultation with an advisory committee, and are intended to take sixty days from inception to publication. The committee serves as a sounding board and provides feedback on a draft report. It usually meets twice— once before a draft is written and once again when there is a draft for review; however, advisory committee members, unlike Task Force members, are not asked to sign off on the report or to otherwise endorse it. Once published, CSRs are posted on www.cfr.org.

For further information about CFR or this Special Report, please write to the Council on Foreign Relations, 58 East 68th Street, New York, NY 10065, or call the Communications office at 212.434.9888. Visit our website, CFR.org.

To submit a letter in response to a Council Special Report for publication on our website, CFR.org, you may send an email to CSReditor@cfr.org. Alternatively, letters may be mailed to us at: Publications Department, Council on Foreign Relations, 58 East 68th Street, New York, NY 10065. Letters should include the writer's name, postal address, and daytime phone number. Letters may be edited for length and clarity, and may be published online. Please do not send attachments. All letters become the property of the Council on Foreign Relations and will not be returned. We regret that, owing to the volume of correspondence, we cannot respond to every letter.

This report is printed on paper that is FSC® certified by Rainforest Alliance, which promotes environmentally responsible, socially beneficial, and economically viable management of the world's forests.

Contents

Foreword

Over the last ten years, drones have become a critical tool in the war against terrorist and militant organizations worldwide. Their advantages over other weapons and intelligence systems are well known. They can silently observe an individual, group, or location for hours on end, but take immediate action should a strike opportunity become available—all without putting a pilot at risk. This combination of capabilities is unique and has allowed the United States to decimate the leadership of al-Qaeda in Afghanistan and disrupt the activities of many other militant groups.

Yet, as Micah Zenko writes in this Council Special Report, drones are not without their drawbacks, especially with regard to targeted killings. Like any tool, drones are only as useful as the information guiding them, and for this they are heavily reliant on local military and intelligence cooperation. More important, significant questions exist about who constitutes a legitimate target and under what circumstances it is acceptable to strike. There is also the question of net utility: To what extent are the specific benefits derived from drone strikes offset by the reality that the strikes often alienate the local government and population? And there is the reality that drones are proliferating but, as is often the case with new technologies, the international legal and regulatory framework is lagging behind.

Zenko puts forward a substantive agenda. He argues that the United States should end so-called signature strikes, which target unidentified militants based on their behavior patterns and personal networks, and limit targeted killings to a limited number of specific terrorists with transnational ambitions. He also calls Congress to improve its oversight of drone strikes and to continue restrictions on armed drone sales. Finally, he recommends that the United States work internationally to establish rules and norms governing the use of drones.

Reforming U.S. Drone Strike Policies raises an important and under-examined set of issues. It analyzes the potentially serious consequences, both at home and abroad, of a lightly overseen drone program and makes recommendations for improving its governance. The result is a provocative report that is well worth reading and contemplating.

Richard N. Haass
President
Council on Foreign Relations
January 2013

Acknowledgments

I would like to express my gratitude to the many people who made this report possible. To begin, thank you to CFR President Richard N. Haass and Director of Studies James M. Lindsay for providing the opportunity to write this report, and for their insightful feedback on multiple drafts.

The report's advisory committee was an invaluable resource. In particular, I am grateful to advisory committee members who went above and beyond the call of duty—namely, Ashley Deeks, Matthew Waxman, Sarah E. Kreps, John B. Bellinger III, David Rohde, Sarah Holewinski, General Stanley A. McChrystal, and Noah Shachtman. I owe a huge debt of gratitude to David Bradley, who chaired the advisory committee.

The report also benefited from over five dozen interviews conducted with current and former civilian and military officials from the U.S. government, as well as insights from the growing number of researchers, journalists, and activists concerned about the emergence of America's use of drones.

I am also grateful to Patricia Dorff, Lia Norton, and Ashley Bregman in Publications for providing their usual and unmatched editing support, and to Lisa Shields and Melinda Wuellner in Global Communications and Media Relations for their marketing efforts. I appreciate the contributions of the Studies staff, including Anya Schmemann, Amy Baker, and Veronica Chiu, in shepherding the report.

Tremendous thanks are also owed to Sophia Yang and Andrew Miller in the Center for Preventive Action (CPA), and above all to my colleague and CPA Director Paul B. Stares, who provided needed guidance and insights. I am also grateful for the logistical and research support of CPA interns Brandon Smith, Shelly Liu, and Shirlynn Sham, and am especially appreciative of the tireless and essential role filled by

Research Associate Emma Welch, without whom the report would not have been started or completed.

Finally, I am thankful for the edits and comments offered by Georgetown University doctoral candidate Rebecca R. Friedman and my brother, Adam Zenko.

This publication was made possible by a grant from Carnegie Corporation of New York. The statements made and views expressed herein are solely my own.

Micah Zenko

Council Special Report

Introduction

Over the past decade, the use of unmanned aerial systems—commonly referred to as drones—by the U.S. government has expanded exponentially in scope, location, and frequency.[1] From September 2001 to April 2012, the U.S. military increased its drone inventory from fifty to seventy-five hundred—of which approximately 5 percent can be armed.[2] Yet despite the unprecedented escalation of its fleet and missions, the U.S. government has not provided a clear explanation of how drone strikes in nonbattlefield settings are coordinated with broader foreign policy objectives, the scope of legitimate targets, and the legal framework. Drones are critical counterterrorism tools that advance U.S. interests around the globe, but this lack of transparency threatens to limit U.S. freedom of action and risks proliferation of armed drone technology without the requisite normative framework.

Existing practices carry two major risks for U.S. interests that are likely to grow over time. The first comes from operational restrictions on drones due to domestic and international pressure. In the United States, the public and policymakers are increasingly uneasy with limited transparency for targeted killings.[3] If the present trajectory continues, drones may share the fate of Bush-era enhanced interrogation techniques and warrantless wiretapping—the unpopularity and illegality of which eventually caused the policy's demise. Internationally, objections from host states and other counterterrorism partners could also severely circumscribe drones' effectiveness. Host states have grown frustrated with U.S. drone policy, while opposition by nonhost partners could impose additional restrictions on the use of drones. Reforming U.S. drone strike policies can do much to allay concerns internationally by ensuring that targeted killings are defensible under international legal regimes that the United States itself helped establish, and by allowing U.S. officials to openly address concerns and counter misinformation.

The second major risk is that of proliferation. Over the next decade, the U.S. near-monopoly on drone strikes will erode as more countries develop and hone this capability. The advantages and effectiveness of drones in attacking hard-to-reach and time-sensitive targets are compelling many countries to indigenously develop or explore purchasing unmanned aerial systems. In this uncharted territory, U.S. policy provides a powerful precedent for other states and nonstate actors that will increasingly deploy drones with potentially dangerous ramifications. Reforming its practices could allow the United States to regain moral authority in dealings with other states and credibly engage with the international community to shape norms for responsible drone use.

The current trajectory of U.S. drone strike policies is unsustainable. Without reform from within, drones risk becoming an unregulated, unaccountable vehicle for states to deploy lethal force with impunity. Consequently, the United States should more fully explain and reform aspects of its policies on drone strikes in nonbattlefield settings by ending the controversial practice of "signature strikes"; limiting targeted killings to leaders of transnational terrorist organizations and individuals with direct involvement in past or ongoing plots against the United States and its allies; and clarifying rules of the road for drone strikes in nonbattlefield settings. Given that the United States is currently the only country—other than the United Kingdom in the traditional battlefield of Afghanistan and perhaps Israel—to use drones to attack the sovereign territory of another country, it has a unique opportunity and responsibility to engage relevant international actors and shape development of a normative framework for acceptable use of drones.

Although reforming U.S. drone strike policies will be difficult and will require sustained high-level attention to balance transparency with the need to protect sensitive intelligence sources and methods, it would serve U.S. national interests by

- allowing policymakers and diplomats to paint a more accurate portrayal of drones to counter the myths and misperceptions that currently remain unaddressed due to secrecy concerns;
- placing the use of drones as a counterterrorism tactic on a more legitimate and defensible footing with domestic and international audiences;

- increasing the likelihood that the United States will sustain the international tolerance and cooperation required to carry out future drone strikes, such as intelligence support and host-state basing rights;
- exerting a normative influence on the policies and actions of other states; and
- providing current and future U.S. administrations with the requisite political leverage to shape and promote responsible use of drones by other states and nonstate actors.

As Obama administration officials have warned about the proliferation of drones, "If we want other nations to use these technologies responsibly, we must use them responsibly."[4]

How Drones Are Different

The U.S. use of armed drones has two unique advantages over manned aircraft, distant missile strikes, and special operations raids when it comes to destroying targets. First, drones allow for sustained persistence over potential targets. The existing U.S. arsenal of armed drones—primarily the Predator and Reaper—can remain aloft, fully loaded with munitions, for over fourteen hours, compared to four hours or less for F-16 fighter jets and A-10 ground attack aircraft.[5] And unlike manned aircraft or raids, drones fly directly over hostile territory without placing pilots or ground troops at risk of injury, capture, or death.

Second, drones provide a near-instantaneous responsiveness—dramatically shrinking what U.S. military targeting experts call the "find-fix-finish" loop—that most other platforms lack. For example, a drone-fired missile travels faster than the speed of sound, striking a target within seconds—often before it is heard by people on the ground. This ability stands in stark contrast to the August 1998 cruise missile salvo targeting Osama bin Laden, which had to be programmed based on projections of where he would be in four to six hours, to allow time to analyze the intelligence, obtain presidential authorization, program the missiles, and fly them to the target.[6] Intercontinental ballistic missiles (ICBMs) loaded with conventional munitions can reach distant targets much faster than cruise missiles, but they carry the dire risk of misattribution as a U.S. nuclear first strike against Russia or China, for instance. Finally, drone-fired missiles can be—and have been—diverted at the last moment if noncombatants enter the likely blast radius.[7]

Altogether, such advantages result in far less collateral damage from drones than other weapons platforms or special operations raids, according to U.S. military officials.[8] However, drones suffer two limitations. First, the precision and discrimination of drones are only as good as the supporting intelligence, which is derived from multiple sources.

In the tribal areas along the border of Afghanistan and Pakistan, for instance, the Central Intelligence Agency (CIA) reportedly maintains a paramilitary force of three thousand ethnic Pashtuns to capture, kill, and collect intelligence.[9] The CIA and U.S. military also cooperate with their Pakistani counterparts to collect human and signals intelligence to identify and track suspected militants.[10] In addition, the Pakistani army clears the airspace for U.S. drones, and when they inadvertently crash, Pakistani troops have repeatedly fought the Taliban to recover the wreckage.[11] In states without a vast network of enabling intelligence, the CIA or Joint Special Operations Command (JSOC) have significantly less situational awareness and precise targeting information for drones.

Second, U.S. drones have benefited from host-state support, which the United States has helped to secure with extensive side payments in foreign aid and security assistance. The few hundred Predator and Reaper drones that currently conduct distant airstrikes leverage a system-wide infrastructure that includes host-state permission to base drones and associated launch and recovery personnel, overflight rights in transit countries, nearby search-and-rescue forces to recover downed drones, satellites or assured access to commercial satellite bandwidth to transmit command-and-control data, and human intelligence assets on the ground to help identify targets.[12] To this end, the United States takes advantage of relatively permissive environments, largely unthreatened by antiaircraft guns or surface-to-air missiles, in the countries where nonbattlefield targeted killings have occurred. According to Lieutenant General David Deptula, former Air Force deputy chief of staff for intelligence, "Some of the [drones] that we have today, you put in a high-threat environment, and they'll start falling from the sky like rain." In fact, in 1995, relatively unsophisticated Serbian antiaircraft guns shot down two of the first three Predator drones deployed outside of the United States, and Iraqi jet fighters shot down a Predator in 2002.[13] Although the next generation of armed drones should be more resilient, current versions lack the speed, stealth, and decoy capabilities to protect themselves against even relatively simple air defense systems.

The combination of persistence and responsiveness, high-quality intelligence infrastructures, and tacit host-state support have made drones the preeminent tool for U.S. lethal operations against suspected terrorists and militants where states are unable to singlehandedly deal with the threat they pose. As a result, drones are not just another weapons platform. Instead, they provide the United States with a distinct capability that significantly reduces many of the inherent political, diplomatic, and military risks of targeted killings.

Compared to other military tools, the advantages of using drones—particularly, that they avoid direct risks to U.S. servicemembers—vastly outweigh the limited costs and consequences. Decision-makers are now much more likely to use lethal force against a range of perceived threats than in the past. Since 9/11, over 95 percent of all nonbattlefield targeted killings have been conducted by drones—the remaining attacks were JSOC raids and AC-130 gunships and offshore sea- or air-launched cruise missiles. And the frequency of drone strikes is only increasing over time. George W. Bush authorized more nonbattlefield targeted killing strikes than any of his predecessors (50), and Barack Obama has more than septupled that number since he entered office (350). Yet without any meaningful checks—imposed by domestic or international political pressure—or sustained oversight from other branches of government, U.S. drone strikes create a moral hazard because of the negligible risks from such strikes and the unprecedented disconnect between American officials and personnel and the actual effects on the ground.[14] However, targeted killings by other platforms would almost certainly inflict greater collateral damage, and the effectiveness of drones makes targeted killings the more likely policy option compared to capturing suspected militants or other nonmilitary options.

Drone strikes outside of defined battlefields are inherently difficult to assess and analyze. Programs and missions are highly classified. Unlike other controversial counterterrorism programs that expanded in the wake of 9/11, the Bush administration never openly discussed any aspects of its targeted killing policies. In comparison, the Obama administration has been much more transparent, beginning with its first official acknowledgment of the practice of targeted killings by drones in April 2012. Nevertheless, strikes by the CIA remain covert, defined by law as "an activity or activities . . . where it is intended that the role of the United States Government will not be apparent or acknowledged publicly," while drone strikes conducted by JSOC in Yemen or Somalia are publicly reported to Congress as "direct actions," albeit with no specificity.[15]

Issues in U.S. Drone Strike Policies

There are four critical issues confronting U.S. drone strike policies: coordination with broader U.S. foreign policy objectives, signature strikes and civilian casualties, transparency and oversight, and legality.

COORDINATION WITH BROADER U.S. FOREIGN POLICY OBJECTIVES

The Obama administration argues that drone strikes are only one tool of national power that is carefully integrated into broader foreign policy objectives. For example, operations conducted by JSOC are "coordinated" with the local U.S. ambassador and fall under the command of the regional combatant commander. Drone strikes conducted by the CIA in nonbattlefield settings are not similarly coordinated, however, and successive U.S. ambassadors to Pakistan have objected to the intensity and timing of certain CIA drone strikes.[16]

The articulated objective of the U.S. counterterrorism strategy is to destroy and eliminate al-Qaeda from "Afghanistan, Pakistan, Yemen, Africa, and other areas," according to White House senior counterterrorism adviser John Brennan.[17] In a narrow military sense, drone strikes have proven effective in achieving their initial objective: killing suspected "high-value" al-Qaeda leaders. In 2009, CIA director Leon Panetta observed that drones are "the only game in town in terms of confronting or trying to disrupt the al-Qaeda leadership," which remains the position of the Obama administration.[18] By December 2011, President Obama boasted, "twenty-two out of thirty top al-Qaeda leaders [have] been taken off the battlefield"—all but Osama bin Laden via drone strikes. In one of his final letters to his followers, bin Laden warned of "the importance of the exit from Waziristan of the brother leaders . . . and that you choose distant locations to which to move them, away from aircraft photography and bombardment."[19] Altogether, U.S. drone strikes in Pakistan, Yemen, and Somalia have significantly degraded the capability of al-Qaeda to plan or conduct acts of international terrorism.

From a strategic perspective, however, it remains unclear if drone strikes are successful or sustainable. There is a clear disconnect between whom the Obama administration claims to target with drones and who has actually been killed. According to U.S. officials, individuals targeted by drones are limited to "high-level al-Qaeda leaders who are planning attacks"; "individuals who are a threat to the United States"; individuals involved in "some sort of operational plot against the United States"; and "specific senior operational leaders of al-Qaeda and associated forces."[20] Of the estimated three thousand people killed by drones, however, the vast majority were neither al-Qaeda nor Taliban leaders. Instead, most were low-level, anonymous suspected militants who were predominantly engaged in insurgent or terrorist operations against their governments, rather than in active international terrorist plots.[21] By targeting individuals who are not terrorist leaders and who do not pose a direct threat to the United States or its allies—but are predominantly fighting insurgent operations—the United States risks being dragged further into internal armed struggles, because it is explicitly intervening on behalf of the government.

Some former and current U.S. officials maintain that the United States relies too much on drone strikes at the expense of longer-term strategies to prevent conditions that foster international terrorism.[22] At best, targeted killings appear to be a stalemate. By some accounts, however, drone strikes may be indirectly increasing the number of militants. In Yemen, for example, in 2010 the Obama administration described al-Qaeda in the Arabian Peninsula (AQAP) as encompassing "several hundred al-Qaeda members"; two years later, it increased to "more than a thousand members." By July 2012, AQAP had "a few thousand members."[23] The evidence that U.S. drone strikes create "blowback"—whereby killing suspected militants or civilians leads to the marked radicalization of local populations that join or sympathize with al-Qaeda or affiliated organizations—varies widely within the affected states, and it is difficult to determine motivations for joining domestic insurgencies and groups dedicated primarily to international terrorism like AQAP, which has made several attempts to attack the United

States. Nevertheless, there appears to be a strong correlation in Yemen between increased targeted killings since December 2009 and heightened anger toward the United States and sympathy with or allegiance to AQAP.[24]

At the same time, some drone strikes contradict stated nonmilitary foreign policy objectives. In February 2012, at a press conference for the International Contact Group on Somalia, Secretary of State Hillary Clinton remarked: "I know enough to say airstrikes would not be a good idea. And we have absolutely no reason to believe anyone—certainly not the United States—is considering that."[25] Within hours, a convoy was attacked in the Shabelle region of Somalia, killing between four and seven suspected Islamic militants.[26] An anonymous U.S. official confirmed that a JSOC drone killed the militants.[27]

Even where military commands are responsible for advancing U.S. interests within a region, coordination with other military branches and the CIA or JSOC is negligible, according to current and former intelligence and military officials. Lieutenant General Sam Helland, who led Combined Joint Task Force–Horn of Africa from 2004 to 2005, described the division as such: "[It was like] the separation of church and state—they were state, I was church. [The CIA and JSOC] did what they did. . . . We stayed on the civil affairs side, drilling wells, building roads, schoolhouses, churches."[28]

In countries where drone strikes have occurred, some State Department and U.S. Agency for International Development (USAID) officials strongly believe that the broadly unpopular attacks overshadow and diminish the effectiveness of civilian assistance programs. One former senior military official closely involved in U.S. targeted killings argued that "drone strikes are just a signal of arrogance that will boomerang against America," while former U.S. ambassador to Pakistan Cameron Munter explained, "The problem is the political fallout. . . . Do you want to win a few battles and lose the war?"[29] In Pakistan, the continuation of drone strikes has exposed fault lines between the army and the democratically elected parliament, which in April 2012 demanded "an immediate cessation of drone attacks inside the territorial borders of Pakistan."[30] However, the central governments of Yemen and Somalia (as represented by the Transitional Federal Government) have provided either public or private consent for U.S. drone strikes within their territories.

SIGNATURE STRIKES
AND CIVILIAN CASUALTIES

Whereas previously President George W. Bush had only permitted the targeted killing of specific individuals, in 2008 he authorized the practice of so-called signature drone strikes against suspected al-Qaeda and Taliban fighters in Pakistan. Also termed "crowd killing" or terrorist attack disruption strikes by CIA officials, signature strikes target anonymous suspected militants "that bear the characteristics of Qaeda or Taliban leaders on the run."[31] President Obama extended and expanded this practice into Yemen, which "in effect counts all military-age males in a strike zone as combatants . . . unless there is explicit intelligence posthumously proving them innocent."[32] Human rights advocates, international legal experts, and current and former U.S. officials dispute whether this post hoc methodology meets the principle of distinction for the use of lethal force.

In addition to targeting individuals on "kill lists" vetted by an opaque interagency process and nearby military-age males, U.S. drone strikes have also killed innocent civilians. In a few instances, civilians were knowingly killed when a senior member of al-Qaeda was the intended target, although the vast majority of collateral deaths were unintentional. The U.S. military has a collateral damage estimate methodology—known as the "bug splat"—which the CIA also employs, according to former senior intelligence officials. Despite what Air Force and intelligence officials describe as rigorous methodology, various U.S. government estimates of cumulative civilian casualties range from zero to sixty.[33] It is unclear if JSOC maintains a similar or different method for compiling civilian casualties, but according to a Pentagon spokesperson, "We're very confident that the number is very low."[34] Estimates of civilian casualties from drone strikes by research organizations are presented in Table 1. These estimates—based on publicly available news reports—are between two and ten times higher than those provided by U.S. government officials, and are further complicated by the fact that some groups targeted by drones purposefully operate out of civilian facilities in an effort to avoid being killed; by the lack of reliable direct access for journalists due to threats from governments or nonstate actors; and by the Islamic practice of washing, wrapping, and burying an individual on the date of death.

TABLE 1: ESTIMATES OF U.S. DRONE STRIKES AND FATALITIES

Source/Year	Number of Strikes	Total Killed	Number of Civilians Killed	Percentage of Civilians Killed
Pakistan				
NAF	340	2,572	175	7
2004–2007	10	178	101	58
2008	36	282	25	10
2009	54	536	25	6
2010	122	818	14	2
2011	72	483	6	1
2012	46	277	5	2
LWJ	325	2,592	142	5
2004	1			
2005	1			
2006	3	142	20	14
2007	5	73	0	0
2008	35	317	31	10
2009	53	506	43	9
2010	117	815	14	2
2011	64	435	30	7
2012	46	304	4	1
TBIJ	358	3,019	681	23
Yemen				
NAF	42	655	44	7
LWJ	59	386	82	21
2002	1	6	0	0
2009	2	55	41	74
2010	4	16	6	37
2011	10	81	0	0
2012	42	228	35	16
TBIJ	59	724	122	17
Somalia				
TBIJ	17	114	34	30
Est. Total*	**411**	**3,430**	**450**	**13**

Sources: New America Foundation (NAF); Long War Journal (LWJ); The Bureau of Investigative Journalism (TBIJ)

*Based on averages within the ranges provided by the organizations monitoring each country through December 2012.

Obama administration officials have also failed to address other troubling questions about the scope of drone strikes. For instance, do legitimate targets include children, individuals attempting to rescue drone strike victims, and the funeral processions of deceased militants? U.S. drones have reportedly targeted all three on multiple occasions.[35] Presumably, the United States deliberately targets these groups, but when asked, U.S. officials will not acknowledge such practices. In addition, it is unclear if there is a process in place to investigate accidental civilian casualties, hold willful perpetrators of those actions accountable, or provide compensation to the families of unintended victims—similar to the process for accidental civilian casualties as a result of U.S. military operations in Afghanistan. (Some families or tribes that suffered the effects of collateral damage from U.S. targeted killings claim that they received compensation from the host state, while others have not.) None of these targeting issues stems directly from drones themselves, but instead from the policy choices about how targets are selected, public articulation of who is targeted, and the maintained position that highly publicized CIA drone strikes are covert and thus cannot be acknowledged.

TRANSPARENCY AND OVERSIGHT

Breaking with precedent, the Obama administration began to acknowledge the broad outlines of select drone strikes in early 2012. Initially, the Obama administration maintained that all targeted killings in non-battlefield settings were classified as covert, and officials refused to admit their existence on the record while candidly discussing the strikes off the record. But in January 2012, President Obama unexpectedly answered a pointed question about drones: "A lot of these strikes have been in the FATA [Federally Administered Tribal Areas of Pakistan] going after al-Qaeda suspects . . . actually, drones have not caused a huge amount of civilian casualties."[36] His unprecedented candor was closely followed by a succession of major policy speeches by Attorney General Eric Holder, John Brennan, and the general counsels of the Pentagon and the State Department discussing some of the legal and political principles that apply to U.S. counterterrorism operations. This progress was short lived, however; President Obama and senior administration officials have subsequently refused to clarify lingering questions about drone strikes, and have instead invited journalists and researchers to reread the earlier policy speeches.

The problem with maintaining that drone strikes are covert is that both the American and international publics often misunderstand how drones are used. And in affected states, citizens often blame the United States for collateral damage that could have been caused by the host states' own weapon systems. According to a recent report from Yemen:

> It's extremely difficult to figure out who is responsible for any given strike. . . . It could be a manned plane from the Yemeni Air Force or the U.S. military. Or it could be an unmanned drone flown by the U.S. military or the CIA. . . . But no matter who launches a particular strike, Yemenis are likely to blame it on the Americans. What's more, we found that many more civilians are being killed than officials acknowledge.[37]

Congressional oversight of drone strikes varies depending on whether the CIA or the U.S. military is the lead executive authority. The CIA, according to the chair of the Senate Select Committee on Intelligence, Senator Dianne Feinstein, meets its "fully and currently informed" legal obligations through "monthly in-depth oversight meetings to review strike records and question every aspect of the program."[38] Individual JSOC strikes are not reported to the relevant armed services committees, but are covered under the broad special access program biannual reporting to Congress. According to senior staff members on the Senate Foreign Relations Committee and House Foreign Affairs Committee, many of their peers have little understanding of how drone strikes are conducted within the countries for which they are responsible for exercising oversight. Even serving White House officials and members of Congress repeatedly make inaccurate statements about U.S. targeted killings and appear to be unaware of how policies have changed over the past decade.[39] At the same time, the judiciary committees have been repeatedly denied access to the June 2010 Office of Legal Counsel memorandum that presented the legal basis for the drone strike that killed U.S. citizen and alleged leader of AQAP Anwar al-Awlaki in September 2011.[40] Finally, despite nearly ten years of nonbattlefield targeted killings, no congressional committee has conducted a hearing on any aspect of them.

LEGALITY

The Obama administration contends that its practice of targeted killings in nonbattlefield settings is consistent with all applicable domestic and international laws. The domestic rationale is based on the
Authorization for the Use of Military Force (AUMF) joint resolution
that was passed by Congress on September 18, 2001, which authorizes
the president

> [t]o use all necessary and appropriate force against those nations,
> organizations, or persons he determines planned, authorized,
> committed, or aided the terrorist attacks that occurred on Sep-
> tember 11, 2001, or harbored such organizations or persons, in
> order to prevent any future acts of international terrorism against
> the United States by such nations, organizations or persons.[41]

Based on the interpretation of the AUMF by the Obama administration, the scope of targets includes individuals who are part of al-Qaeda,
the Taliban, or associated forces, whether they are located on "hot"
battlefields like Afghanistan, or somewhere else. Though the Obama
administration takes the legal position that targeted killings do not
require "a separate self-defense analysis each time," it similarly claims
that each legitimate target must pose "an imminent threat of violent
attack against the United States."[42] According to Director of National
Intelligence James Clapper, the same legal rationale applies to all U.S.
counterterrorism operations, regardless of whether the lead executive
authority is the CIA or JSOC. However, some legal scholars argue that,
since the death of Osama bin Laden and decimation of al-Qaeda, the
White House should seek congressional approval beyond the post-9/11
AUMF to conduct drone strikes in Yemen and Somalia.[43]
     The Obama administration offers several international legal justi-
fications for U.S. drone strikes that stem from the assertion that the
United States is in a continuous state of international armed conflict
with al-Qaeda and associated forces. As a result, the laws of armed
conflict (or international humanitarian law) apply, including necessity,
proportionality, distinction, and humanity. The Obama administration
argues that the treaty provisions of the International Covenant on Civil
and Political Rights, of which the United States is a signatory, applies
only to persons within the United States.[44]

In defense of sovereignty violations, American officials contend that the United States is exercising its inherent right to self-defense under Article 51 of the United Nations (UN) charter by using lethal force when a targeted country is unable or unwilling to counter imminent and significant threats. What remains unclear to many legal scholars is to what degree international humanitarian law and/or human rights law should apply. U.S. officials will not state if they do, but maintain that the two bodies of law are complementary and reinforcing.[45] Although no other countries have publicly condoned the U.S. international legal justification of drone strikes, they also have refrained from raising the issue of targeted killings in relevant forums such as the UN Human Rights Council.

The UN special rapporteur on extrajudicial, summary, or arbitrary executions repeatedly requests information about U.S. nonbattlefield targeted killings, including what international laws apply, whether the targeted states provide consent, and which specific procedural safeguards are in place. Although Pentagon, State Department, and CIA legal officials routinely discuss counterterrorism policies with the special rapporteur, the official U.S. position is that "inquiries related to allegations stemming from military operations conducted during the course of an armed conflict with Al Qaida do not fall within the mandate of the Special Rapporteur."[46] The special rapporteur recently warned that drone strikes intentionally targeting civilians—including individuals rescuing victims of prior drone strikes or simply attending funerals—would likely constitute war crimes.[47] Like all other signature strikes, the Obama administration will not acknowledge or defend this practice.

Drone Strikes by Other States
or Nonstate Actors

The fact that drones lower the threshold for the use of force, combined with the U.S. justification for the scope of legitimate targets, creates a precedent that other states and nonstate actors could eventually adopt for drone strikes. For the foreseeable future, however, the U.S. military will be the unrivaled leader in developing medium-altitude long-endurance (MALE) armed drone technology; it is projected to account for 62 percent of all drone research and development and 55 percent of all procurement over the next decade.[48] With a projected $80 billion in global spending over the next ten years, drones constitute a potential growth industry for the aerospace and defense sectors. Nevertheless, there is not yet public evidence of non-U.S. states—except Israel—developing an armed drone capability.

STATE ACTORS

It is estimated that the number of states that have acquired a complete drone system has grown from forty-one in 2005 to seventy-six in 2012.[49] Over that same period of time, the number of total drone programs within those states increased from one hundred ninety-five to nine hundred.[50] Like the United States, the vast majority of all drones developed by other countries will be used exclusively for government or civilian intelligence, surveillance, and reconnaissance (ISR) missions. Some advanced industrial economies—such as Russia, Taiwan, and South Korea—have developed increasingly sophisticated and largely indigenous drone capabilities, but they have also missed deadlines for when they would field armed drones, according to their own defense ministries. There is no international association for drone manufacturers and operators—similar to those that exist for civilian nuclear facilities or commercial space launches—that provides reliable information on drones or serves as a forum to exchange best practices to limit the associated risks and costs. Since most publicly available information is limited to air shows and the defense trade press, it is possible that there have been intentionally hidden advances toward states' development of weaponized drones.

Russian armed forces currently do not have armed drones, although the Ministry of Defense signed contracts with domestic aerospace firms to build a prototype by 2014, with the goal of the drones entering service by 2020.[51] Russia claims to have developed the Lutch, an armed drone capable of holding 350 pounds of munitions and remaining aloft for eighteen hours, although there are no known sales.[52] China is investing in drone programs, with at least twenty-five prototypes in development, including armed variants potentially for export. A Chinese aerospace spokesperson remarked, "The United States doesn't export many attack drones, so we're taking advantage of that hole in the market."[53] However, Chinese displays at air shows have been limited to models and computer graphics. Little is known about the Chinese program; according to a recent Pentagon report, "Data on the actual extent of [drone] production is nearly non-existent, and there is little available information on China's overall procurement objectives."[54] Iran also touts its nascent program, but most of its drones are extremely crude and primarily used for antiaircraft target practice. Several of Iran's more capable spy drones, like the Ababil III, were easily tracked down over Iraq by U.S. fighter jets.[55] Iran also claims to have fielded an armed drone called the Ambassador of Death, which would effectively function as an imprecise one-time-only cruise missile.

In the absence of an indigenous armed drone capacity, interested states are looking to buy. Thus far, the United States has refrained from selling armed drones to states, such as Pakistan, Turkey, Saudi Arabia, and the United Arab Emirates (UAE), that have requested the technology, though it has made exceptions for Great Britain and possibly Italy. U.S. aerospace companies have lobbied to relax the export regulations for drones, primarily those that conduct surveillance missions.[56] One hurdle is that the United States is a member of the 1987 Missile Technology Control Regime (MTCR), an informal and voluntary multilateral arrangement comprising thirty-four states that attempts to constrain ballistic missile proliferation. Under the MTCR, drones capable of delivering at least a five-hundred-kilogram payload a minimum of three hundred kilometers are classified as Category I items, for which "there will be a strong presumption to deny such transfers." So far, the United States has largely followed the Category I guidelines. General Atomics, manufacturer of the Predator, recently unveiled the Predator XP surveillance drone, which lacks the hard points—or mounting brackets for aerial munitions—wing strength, and fire control system required for weaponization.

There are also few examples of armed drone sales by other countries. After the United States, Israel has the most developed and varied drone capabilities; according to the Stockholm International Peace Research Institute (SIPRI), Israel was responsible for 41 percent of drones exported between 2001 and 2011.[57] While Israel has used armed drones in the Palestinian territories and is not a member of the MTCR, it has predominantly sold surveillance drones that lack hard points and electrical engineering. Israel reportedly sold the Harop, a short-range attack drone, to France, Germany, Turkey, and India. Furthermore, Israel allows the United States to veto transfers of weapons with U.S.-origin technology to select states, including China.[58] Other states invested in developing and selling surveillance drones have reportedly refrained from selling fully armed versions. For example, the UAE spent five years building the armed United-40 drone with an associated Namrod missile, but there have been no reported deliveries.[59] A March 2011 analysis by the marketing research firm Lucintel projected that a "fully developed [armed drone] product will take another decade."[60]

Based on current trends, it is unlikely that most states will have, within ten years, the complete system architecture required to carry out distant drone strikes that would be harmful to U.S. national interests. However, those candidates able to obtain this technology will most likely be states with the financial resources to purchase or the industrial base to manufacture tactical short-range armed drones with limited firepower that lack the precision of U.S. laser-guided munitions; the intelligence collection and military command-and-control capabilities needed to deploy drones via line-of-sight communications; and cross-border adversaries who currently face attacks or the threat of attacks by manned aircraft, such as Israel into Lebanon, Egypt, or Syria; Russia into Georgia or Azerbaijan; Turkey into Iraq; and Saudi Arabia into Yemen. When compared to distant U.S. drone strikes, these contingencies do not require system-wide infrastructure and host-state support. Given the costs to conduct manned-aircraft strikes with minimal threat to pilots, it is questionable whether states will undertake the significant investment required for armed drones in the near term.

NONSTATE ACTORS

Though industry, researchers, hobbyists, and activists have been at the forefront of drone innovation, few nonstate actors with a history of acting against U.S. interests have developed armed drones. Among the few groups that have used drones, the leader is Hezbollah, which has flown the Iranian-supplied Abibil that reportedly boasts an eighty-eight-pound explosive triggered by crashing the drone into a target. In 2006, Israel easily shot down several such drones with fighter jets.[61] Given that Hezbollah reportedly has over sixty thousand rockets and missiles of varying degrees of accuracy, drones would provide little additional attack capability.[62]

Other nonstate actors could easily carry out similar terrorist attacks with explosives-laden drones, but that would inflict little damage. In July 2012, for example, U.S. citizen Rezwan Ferdaus pleaded guilty to two counts: attempting to damage and destroy a federal building, and attempting to provide material support to terrorists. Ferdaus plotted to attack the Pentagon and U.S. Capitol with three remotely piloted aircraft, ranging from sixty to eighty inches in length, with a wingspan between forty-four and sixty-three inches. Each of the drones would have been directed to their targets via Global Positioning System (GPS) coordinates laden with five pounds of homemade explosives, which would cause insignificant damage to either building.

Given their size, weight, and power limitations, primitive drones like those Ferdaus sought to build could become more prevalent in domestic terror attacks and against U.S. bases or diplomatic outposts abroad. They would likely contain amounts of explosive similar to that of a suicide attack, but certainly less than that found in a typical car bomb. Moreover, the United States does not face a plausible or imminent threat of armed drone attack on the U.S. homeland.

Recommendations

In his Nobel Peace Prize acceptance speech, President Obama declared: "Where force is necessary, we have a moral and strategic interest in binding ourselves to certain rules of conduct. Even as we confront a vicious adversary that abides by no rules, I believe the United States of America must remain a standard bearer in the conduct of war."[63] Under President Obama drone strikes have expanded and intensified, and they will remain a central component of U.S. counterterrorism operations for at least another decade, according to U.S. officials.[64] But much as the Bush administration was compelled to reform its controversial counterterrorism practices, it is likely that the United States will ultimately be forced by domestic and international pressure to scale back its drone strike policies. The Obama administration can preempt this pressure by clearly articulating that the rules that govern its drone strikes, like all uses of military force, are based in the laws of armed conflict and international humanitarian law; by engaging with emerging drone powers; and, most important, by matching practice with its stated policy by limiting drone strikes to those individuals it claims are being targeted (which would reduce the likelihood of civilian casualties since the total number of strikes would significantly decrease).

The choice the United States faces is not between unfettered drone use and sacrificing freedom of action, but between drone policy reforms by design or drone policy reforms by default. Recent history demonstrates that domestic political pressure could severely limit drone strikes in ways that the CIA or JSOC have not anticipated. In support of its counterterrorism strategy, the Bush administration engaged in the extraordinary rendition of terrorist suspects to third countries, the use of enhanced interrogation techniques, and warrantless wiretapping. Although the Bush administration defended its policies as critical to protecting the U.S. homeland against terrorist attacks, unprecedented domestic political pressure led to significant reforms or termination.

Compared to Bush-era counterterrorism policies, drone strikes are vulnerable to similar—albeit still largely untapped—moral outrage, and they are even more susceptible to political constraints because they occur in plain sight. Indeed, a negative trend in U.S. public opinion on drones is already apparent. Between February and June 2012, U.S. support for drone strikes against suspected terrorists fell from 83 percent to 62 percent—which represents less U.S. support than enhanced interrogation techniques maintained in the mid-2000s.[65] Finally, U.S. drone strikes are also widely opposed by the citizens of important allies, emerging powers, and the local populations in states where strikes occur.[66] States polled reveal overwhelming opposition to U.S. drone strikes: Greece (90 percent), Egypt (89 percent), Turkey (81 percent), Spain (76 percent), Brazil (76 percent), Japan (75 percent), and Pakistan (83 percent).[67]

This is significant because the United States cannot conduct drone strikes in the most critical corners of the world by itself. Drone strikes require the tacit or overt support of host states or neighbors. If such states decided not to cooperate—or to actively resist—U.S. drone strikes, their effectiveness would be immediately and sharply reduced, and the likelihood of civilian casualties would increase. This danger is not hypothetical. In 2007, the Ethiopian government terminated its U.S. military presence after public revelations that U.S. AC-130 gunships were launching attacks from Ethiopia into Somalia. Similarly, in late 2011, Pakistan evicted all U.S. military and intelligence drones, forcing the United States to completely rely on Afghanistan to serve as a staging ground for drone strikes in Pakistan. The United States could attempt to lessen the need for tacit host-state support by making significant investments in armed drones that can be flown off U.S. Navy ships, conducting electronic warfare or missile attacks on air defenses, allowing downed drones to not be recovered and potentially transferred to China or Russia, and losing access to the human intelligence networks on the ground that are critical for identifying targets.

According to U.S. diplomats and military officials, active resistance—such as the Pakistani army shooting down U.S. armed drones—is a legitimate concern. In this case, the United States would need to either end drone sorties or escalate U.S. military involvement by attacking Pakistani radar and antiaircraft sites, thus increasing the likelihood of civilian casualties.[68] Beyond where drone strikes currently take place, political pressure could severely limit options for new U.S. drone bases.

For example, the Obama administration is debating deploying armed drones to attack al-Qaeda in the Islamic Maghreb (AQIM) in North Africa, which would likely require access to a new airbase in the region. To some extent, anger at U.S. sovereignty violations is an inevitable and necessary trade-off when conducting drone strikes. Nevertheless, in each of these cases, domestic anger would partially or fully abate if the United States modified its drone policy in the ways suggested below.

The United States will inevitably improve and enhance the lethal capabilities of its drones. Although many of its plans are classified, the U.S. military has nonspecific objectives to replace the Predators and Reapers with the Next-Generation Remotely Piloted Aircraft (RPA) sometime in the early-to-mid 2020s. Though they are only in the early stages of development, the next generation of armed drones will almost certainly have more missiles of varying types, enhanced guidance and navigation systems, greater durability in the face of hostile air defense environments, and increased maximum loiter time—and even the capability to be refueled in the air by unmanned tankers.[69] Currently, a senior official from the lead executive authority approves U.S. drone strikes in nonbattlefield settings. Several U.S. military and civilian officials claim that there are no plans to develop autonomous drones that can use lethal force. Nevertheless, armed drones will incrementally integrate varying degrees of operational autonomy to overcome their most limiting and costly factor—the human being.[70]

Beyond the United States, drones are proliferating even as they are becoming increasingly sophisticated, lethal, stealthy, resilient, and autonomous. At least a dozen other states and nonstate actors could possess armed drones within the next ten years and leverage the technology in unforeseen and harmful ways. It is the stated position of the Obama administration that its strategy toward drones will be emulated by other states and nonstate actors. In an interview, President Obama revealed, "I think creating a legal structure, processes, with oversight checks on how we use unmanned weapons is going to be a challenge for me and for my successors for some time to come—partly because technology may evolve fairly rapidly for other countries as well."[71]

History shows that how states adopt and use new military capabilities is often influenced by how other states have—or have not—used them in the past. Furthermore, norms can deter states from acquiring new technologies.[72] Norms—sometimes but not always codified as legal regimes—have dissuaded states from deploying blinding lasers and landmines, as well as chemical, biological, and nuclear weapons. A well-articulated and internationally supported normative framework, bolstered by a strong U.S. example, can shape armed drone proliferation and employment in the coming decades. Such norms would not hinder U.S. freedom of action; rather, they would internationalize already-necessary domestic policy reforms and, of course, they would be acceptable only insofar as the limitations placed reciprocally on U.S. drones furthered U.S. objectives. And even if hostile states do not accept norms regulating drone use, the existence of an international normative framework, and U.S. compliance with that framework, would preserve Washington's ability to apply diplomatic pressure. Models for developing such a framework would be based in existing international laws that emphasize the principles of necessity, proportionality, and distinction—to which the United States claims to adhere for its drone strikes—and should be informed by comparable efforts in the realms of cyber and space.

In short, a world characterized by the proliferation of armed drones—used with little transparency or constraint—would undermine core U.S. interests, such as preventing armed conflict, promoting human rights, and strengthening international legal regimes. It would be a world in which targeted killings occur with impunity against anyone deemed an "enemy" by states or nonstate actors, without accountability for legal justification, civilian casualties, and proportionality. Perhaps more troubling, it would be a world where such lethal force no longer heeds the borders of sovereign states. Because of drones' inherent advantages over other weapons platforms, states and nonstate actors would be much more likely to use lethal force against the United States and its allies.

Much like policies governing the use of nuclear weapons, offensive cyber capabilities, and space, developing rules and frameworks for innovative weapons systems, much less reaching a consensus within the U.S. government, is a long and arduous process. In its second term, the Obama administration has a narrow policy window of opportunity to pursue reforms of the targeted killings program. The Obama administration can proactively shape U.S. and international use of armed drones in nonbattlefield settings through transparency, self-restraint, and engagement, or it can continue with its current policies and risk the consequences. To better secure the ability to conduct drone strikes, and potentially influence how others will use armed drones in the future, the United States should undertake the following specific policy recommendations.

EXECUTIVE BRANCH

The president of the United States should

- limit targeted killings to individuals who U.S. officials claim are being targeted—the leadership of al-Qaeda and affiliated forces or individuals with a direct operational role in past or ongoing terrorist plots against the United States and its allies—and bring drone strike practices in line with stated policies;
- either end the practice of signature strikes or provide a public accounting of how it meets the principles of distinction and proportionality that the Obama administration claims;
- review its current policy whereby the executive authority for drone strikes is split between the CIA and JSOC, as each has vastly different legal authorities, degrees of permissible transparency, and oversight;
- provide information to the public, Congress, and UN special rapporteurs—without disclosing classified information—on what procedures exist to prevent harm to civilians, including collateral damage mitigation, investigations into collateral damage, corrective actions based on those investigations, and amends for civilian losses; and
- never conduct nonbattlefield targeted killings without an accountable human being authorizing the strike (while retaining the potential necessity of autonomous decisions to use lethal force *in warfare* in response to ground-based antiaircraft fire or aerial combat).

U.S. CONGRESS

The relevant Senate and House committees should

- demand regular White House briefings on drone strikes and how such operations are coordinated with broader foreign policy objectives, in order to hold the executive branch accountable for its actions;
- hold hearings with government officials and nongovernmental experts on the short- and long-term effects of U.S. targeted killings;
- hold hearings to assess the geographic and temporal limits of the AUMF and the legal justifications for targeted killings of U.S. citizens;

- maintain the MTCR Category I constraints on the export of armed drones and limit the retrofitting of drones already exported to U.S. allies that allow them to be weaponized; and

- withhold funding and/or subpoena the executive branch if cooperation is not forthcoming.

INTERNATIONAL COOPERATION

The United States should

- promote Track 1.5 or Track 2 discussions on armed drones, similar to dialogues with other countries on the principles and limits of weapons systems such as nuclear weapons or cyberwarfare;

- create an international association of drone manufacturers that includes broad participation with emerging drone powers that could be modeled on similar organizations like the Nuclear Suppliers Group;

- explicitly state which legal principles apply—and do not apply—to drone strikes and the procedural safeguards to ensure compliance to build broader international consensus;

- begin discussions with emerging drone powers for a code of conduct to develop common principles for how armed drones should be used outside a state's territory, which would address issues such as sovereignty, proportionality, distinction, and appropriate legal framework; and

- host discussions in partnership with Israel to engage emerging drone makers on how to strengthen norms against selling weapons-capable systems.

Endnotes

1. Beyond the war zones of Afghanistan, Iraq, and Libya, drones have targeted and killed suspected terrorists and militants in Pakistan, Yemen, Somalia, and possibly the Philippines, and have conducted covert surveillance missions over Iran and North Korea, among others.

2. W. J. Hennigan, "Pentagon Working with FAA to Open U.S. Airspace to Combat Drones," *Los Angeles Times*, February 13, 2012; Jeremiah Gertler, "U.S. Unmanned Aerial Systems," Congressional Research Service, January 3, 2012.

3. *Washington Post*/NBC News Poll, February 2012; Pew Research Center Global Attitudes Project, June 13, 2012.

4. John O. Brennan, "The Ethics and Efficacy of the President's Counterterrorism Strategy," Wilson Center, April 30, 2012.

5. Winslow Wheeler, "The MQ-9's Cost and Performance," *Time*, February 28, 2012.

6. Steve Coll, *Ghost Wars: The Secret History of the CIA, Afghanistan, and bin Laden, from the Soviet Invasion to September 10, 2001*, p. 421; Daniel Benjamin and Steven Simon, *The Age of Sacred Terror*, p. 294.

7. Interview with U.S. officials; Ken Dilanian, "CIA Drones May Be Avoiding Pakistani Civilians," *Los Angeles Times*, February 22, 2011; and Scott Shane, "CIA Is Disputed on Civilian Toll in Drone Strikes," *New York Times*, August 11, 2011.

8. Interviews with current and former U.S. civilian and military officials involved in targeted killings.

9. Bob Woodward, *Obama's Wars*, pp. 106–107; Joby Warrick, *The Triple Agent: The al-Qaeda Mole Who Infiltrated the CIA*, pp. 113–114.

10. Interviews with U.S. officials; Chris Albritton, "Exclusive: How Pakistan Helps the U.S. Drone Campaign," Reuters, January 22, 2012.

11. Karin Brulliard and Haq Nawaz Khan, "Pakistani Officials Say Troops, Taliban Militants Clashed Over Downed Drone," *Washington Post*, September 18, 2011; Jibran Ahmad, "Taliban Militants Say They Shot Down U.S. Drones," Reuters, February 25, 2012; and Adam Entous, Siobhan Gorman, and Evan Perez, "U.S. Unease Over Drone Strikes," *Wall Street Journal*, September 26, 2012.

12. Department of Defense, *Report to Congress on Future Unmanned Aircraft Systems Training, Operations, and Sustainability*, April 2012.

13. James Risen and Ralph Vartabedian, "Spy Plane Woes Create Bosnia Intelligence Gap," *Los Angeles Times*, December 2, 1995; Department of Defense, Press Briefing with Secretary of Defense Donald Rumsfeld and Chairman of the Joint Chiefs of Staff General Richard Myers, December 23, 2002. According to U.S. military officials, the Predator shot down by an Iraqi fighter jet was used in a mission that made it highly likely it would be shot down.

14. Sarah Kreps and John Kaag, "The Moral Hazard of Drones," *New York Times*, July 22, 2012.

15. Office of the White House Press Secretary, "Presidential Letter: 2012 War Powers Resolution 6-Month Report," June 15, 2012.

16. David Ignatius, "An Embassy Asks, Drones or Diplomacy?" *Washington Post*, June 20, 2012.

17. John O. Brennan, *This Week with George Stephanopolous*, ABC, April 29, 2012.

18. "U.S. Airstrikes in Pakistan Called 'Very Effective,'" CNN, May 18, 2009.

19. Don Rassler, Gabriel Koehler-Derrick, Liam Collins, Muhammad al-Obaidi, and Nelly Lahoud, "Letters from Abbottabad: Bin Laden Sidelined?" Combating Terrorism Center, May 3, 2012.

20. Harold Koh, Annual Meeting of the American Society of International Law, March 25, 2012; John O. Brennan, "Strengthening Our Security by Adhering to Our Values and Laws," September 16, 2011; Barack Obama, "Interview on Drone Warfare Use," CNN, September 5, 2012; and Eric Holder, speech at Northwestern University School of Law, March 5, 2012.

21. For example, according to data maintained by the New America Foundation for drone strikes in Pakistan, "Under Bush, about a third of all drone strikes killed a militant leader, compared to less than 13 percent since President Obama took office." Peter Bergen and Megan Braun, "Drone is Obama's Weapon of Choice," CNN, September 5, 2012.

22. Interviews with former and current U.S. officials involved in targeted killings.

23. John Brennan, *State of the Union*, CNN, January 3, 2010; "Brennan on bin Laden Raid, and 'Dangerous' Yemen," CNN Security Clearance, April 20, 2012; and U.S. Department of State, *2011 Country Reports on Terrorism: Foreign Terrorist Organizations*.

24. Jeremy Scahill, "Washington's War in Yemen Backfires," *Nation*, February 14, 2012; Sudarsan Raghavan, "In Yemen, U.S. Airstrikes Breed Anger, and Sympathy for Al Qaeda," *Washington Post*, May 29, 2012; Kelly McEvers, "Yemen Airstrikes Punish Militants, And Civilians," NPR.org, July 6, 2012; Ibrahim Mothama, "How Drones Help Al Qaeda," *New York Times*, June 13, 2012; Gregory D. Johnsen, "The Wrong Man for the CIA," *New York Times*, November 19, 2012.

25. Hillary Rodham Clinton, "Press Availability on the London Conference," February 23, 2012.

26. "Somalia: U.S. Covert Actions 2001-2012," Bureau of Investigative Journalism.

27. "Deaths in U.S. Drone Strike in Somalia," al-Jazeera, February 25, 2012.

28. Sean D. Naylor, "Lack of Human Intel Hampered AQ Hunt in Africa," *Army Times*, November 8, 2011.

29. Interview with former senior U.S. military official, August 2012; Tara McKelvey, "A Former Ambassador to Pakistan Speaks Out," *Daily Beast*, November 20, 2012.

30. *Guidelines for Revised Terms of Engagement with USA/NATO/ISAF and General Foreign Policy*, April 12, 2012.

31. Eric Schmitt and David E. Sanger, "Pakistan Shift Could Curtail Drone Strikes," *New York Times*, February 22, 2008.

32. Adam Entous, Siobhan Gorman, and Julian E. Barnes, "U.S. Relaxes Drone Rules," *Wall Street Journal*, April 26, 2012.

33. Justin Elliott, "Obama Administration's Drone Death Figures Don't Add Up," ProPublica, June 18, 2012.

34. Department of Defense, press briefing with Spokesperson George Little, May 29, 2012.

35. Craig Whitlock, "U.S. Airstrike that Killed American Teen in Yemen Raises Legal, Ethical Questions," *Washington Post*, October 22, 2011; Pir Zubair Shah, "25 Militants are Killed in Attack in Pakistan," *New York Times*, May 16, 2009; Warrick, *The Triple Agent*, pp. 73–74; Scott Shane, "U.S. Said to Target Rescuers at Drone Strike Sites," *New York Times*, February 5, 2012.

36. White House, "President Obama's Google+ Hangout," January 30, 2012.
37. McEvers, July 6, 2012.
38. Dianne Feinstein, "Letters: Senator Feinstein on Drone Strikes," *Los Angeles Times*, May 6, 2012.
39. Hearing Committee on Appropriations, Subcommittee on Commerce, Justice, Science, and Relations Agencies, March 7, 2012; *State of the Union with Candy Crowley*, "Interview with Harry Reid," CNN, March 11, 2012; *This Week with George Stephanopoulos*, "Interview with Charles Schumer," ABC News, March 11, 2012; Robert Naiman, "When a Drone Flies Over Waziristan, Does It Make a Sound?" *Huffington Post*, October 17, 2012.
40. Charlie Savage, "Secret U.S. Memo Made Legal Case to Kill a Citizen," *New York Times*, October 8, 2011. The Office of Legal Counsel memo providing the legal justification for killing Anwar al-Awlaki was completed more than six months after he was placed on a JSOC capture or kill list. Dana Priest, "U.S. Military Teams, Intelligence Deeply Involved in Aiding Yemen on Strikes," *Washington Post*, January 27, 2010.
41. 107th Congress, Authorization for Use of Military Force, September 18, 2001.
42. Brennan, "The Ethics and Efficacy of the President's Counterterrorism Strategy"; Holder, remarks at Northwestern University School of Law, March 5, 2012.
43. Selections from the hearing of the Senate Select Intelligence Committee, "World Wide Threats," January 31, 2012.
44. John B. Bellinger, "Administration Submits ICCPR Report, Punts on Extraterritorial Application," Lawfare, January 19, 2012.
45. Bellinger, "More on the Obama Administration's National Security Speeches," Lawfare, April 20, 2012.
46. Office of the High Commissioner for Human Rights, "Letter from the Chief of Section, Political, and Specialized Agencies of the Permanent Mission of the United States of America," April 22, 2003, p. 2.
47. Owen Bowcott, "Drone Strikes Threaten 50 Years of International Law, Says UN Rapporteur," *Guardian*, June 21, 2012.
48. Steven J. Zaloga, David Rockwell, and Philip Finnegan, "World Unmanned Aerial Vehicle Systems: Market Profile and Forecast," TEAL Group Corporation, June 2012.
49. Government Accountability Office (GAO), *Nonproliferation: Agencies Could Improve Information Sharing and End-Use Monitoring on Unmanned Aerial Vehicles*, July 30, 2012, pp. 9–13.
50. Ibid, p. 13; Jeremiah Gertler, *U.S. Unmanned Aerial Vehicles*, Congressional Research Service, January 3, 2012, p. 28.
51. "Russian Army to Receive First Indigenous Strike UAV in 2014," *Ria Novosti*, June 28, 2012.
52. "First Russian Strike UAV to Be Showcased at Moscow Air Show," *Ria Novosti*, August 10, 2011.
53. William Wan and Peter Finn, "Global Race on to Match U.S. Drone Capabilities," *Washington Post*, July 4, 2011.
54. Defense Science Board, *The Role of Autonomy in DoD Systems*, July 2012, p. 70.
55. Interviews with U.S. military officials; Rod Nordland and Alissa J. Rubin, "U.S. Says It Shot Down an Iranian Drone Over Iraq," *New York Times*, March 16, 2009.
56. Hennigan, "Drone Makers Urge U.S. to Let Them Sell More Overseas," *Los Angeles Times*, July 1, 2012.
57. Stockholm International Peace Research Institute, *Yearbook 2012*.
58. Scott Wilson, "Israel Set to End China Arms Deal Under U.S. Pressure," *Washington Post*, June 27, 2005; David Rosenberg, "Israel-China Relations Growing Deeper," *Jerusalem Post*, July 6, 2012.

59. Ibid; Wikileaks Cable #04ABUDHABI2113, "Shaykh Mohamed bin Zayed Rejects Unarmed Predator Proposal," U.S. Embassy Abu Dhabi, June 27, 2004.

60. *Growth Opportunity in Global UAV Market*, Lucintel, March 2011.

61. Benjamin S. Lambeth, "Air Operations in Israel's War Against Hezbollah," RAND Corporation, 2011, pp. 110–126.

62. Gili Cohen and Jonathan Lis, "IDF: Israel in Range of Nearly 65,000 Hezbollah, Iran, Syria Rockets," *Haaretz*, May 23, 2012.

63. Barack Obama, Remarks by the President at the Acceptance of the Nobel Peace Prize, December 10, 2009.

64. Greg Miller, "Plan for Hunting Terrorists Signals U.S. Intends to Keep Adding Names to Kill Lists," *Washington Post*, October 23, 2012.

65. Washington Post/NBC News Poll, February 2012; Pew Research Center Global Attitudes Project, June 13, 2012.

66. Ibid. The individuals were asked, "Do you approve or disapprove of the United States conducting missile strikes from pilotless aircraft called drones to target extremists in countries such as Pakistan, Yemen and Somalia?" In that survey, 62 percent of Americans approved of drone strikes.

67. Ibid; Pew Research Center Global Attitudes Project, "Pakistani Public Opinion Ever More Critical of U.S.," June 27, 2012.

68. Interviews with former and current U.S. officials involved in targeted killings.

69. Graham Warwick, "Unmanned Tanker," *Aviation Week and Space Technology*, August 13, 2012.

70. Matthew Waxman and Kenneth Anderson, "Law and Ethics for Robot Soldiers," Columbia Public Law Research Paper No. 12-313, April 28, 2012.

71. Mark Bowden, *The Finish* (New York, NY: Atlantic Monthly Press, 2012), p. 262.

72. Ward Thomas, *The Ethics of Destruction: Norms and Force in International Relations* (Ithica, NY: Cornell University Press, 1999); Colin Elman, *The Logic of Emulation: The Diffusion of Military Practices in the International System* (New York, NY: Columbia University Press, 1999); Emily O. Goldman and Leslie C. Eliason, eds., *Diffusion of Military Technology and Ideas* (Palo Alto, CA: Stanford University Press, 2003).

About the Author

Micah Zenko is the Douglas Dillon fellow in the Center for Preventive Action (CPA) at the Council on Foreign Relations (CFR). Previously, he worked for five years at the Harvard Kennedy School and in Washington, DC, at the Brookings Institution, Congressional Research Service, and State Department's Office of Policy Planning.

Zenko has published on a range of national security issues, including articles in *Foreign Affairs*, the *Journal of Strategic Studies*, and *Annals of the American Academy of Political and Social Science*, and op-eds in *Foreign Policy*, the *Washington Post*, *Los Angeles Times*, *Chicago Tribune*, and *New York Times*. He writes the blog Politics, Power, and Preventive Action, which covers U.S. national security policy, international security, and conflict prevention. He tweets at @MicahZenko and was named by *Foreign Policy* as one of the FP Twitterati 100 in 2011 and 2012.

He is the author or coauthor of three previous Council Special Reports: *Partners in Preventive Action: The United States and International Institutions*; *Toward Deeper Reductions in U.S. and Russian Nuclear Weapons*; and *Enhancing U.S. Preventive Action*. His book *Between Threats and War: U.S. Discrete Military Operations in the Post–Cold War World* was published by Stanford University Press. Zenko received a PhD in political science from Brandeis University.

Advisory Committee for
Reforming U.S. Drone Strike Policies

Kenneth Anderson
American University

John B. Bellinger III
Arnold & Porter LLP

David G. Bradley
Atlantic Media Company

Rosa E. Brooks
Georgetown University Law Center

Ashley S. Deeks
University of Virginia School of Law

David Deptula, USAF (Ret.)
U.S. Air Force Academy

Dennis M. Gormley
University of Pittsburgh

Sarah Holewinski
Center for Civilians in Conflict

Sarah Kreps
Cornell University

Daniel S. Markey, *ex officio*
Council on Foreign Relations

Stanley A. McChrystal, USA (Ret.)

Joseph S. Nye Jr.
Harvard University

Paul R. Pillar
Georgetown University

David Rohde
Thomson Reuters

Noah Shachtman
Wired *Magazine*

Paul B. Stares, *ex officio*
Council on Foreign Relations

John Villasenor
University of California, Los Angeles

Andru E. Wall
Alston & Bird, LLP

Matthew C. Waxman, *ex officio*
Council on Foreign Relations

Dov S. Zakheim
Center for Strategic and International Studies

Steven J. Zaloga
Teal Group

CPA Advisory Committee

Peter Ackerman
Rockport Capital, Inc.

Richard K. Betts
Council on Foreign Relations

Patrick M. Byrne
Overstock.com

Leslie H. Gelb
Council on Foreign Relations

Jack A. Goldstone
George Mason University

Sherri W. Goodman
CNA

General George A. Joulwan, USA (Ret.)
One Team, Inc.

Robert S. Litwak
Woodrow Wilson International Center for Scholars

Thomas G. Mahnken
Paul H. Nitze School of Advanced International Studies

Doyle McManus
Los Angeles Times

Susan E. Patricof
Mailman School of Public Health

David Shuman
Northwoods Capital

Nancy E. Soderberg
University of North Florida

General John W. Vessey, USA (Ret.)

Steven D. Winch
The Blackstone Group LP

James D. Zirin
Sidley Austin, LLC

Mission Statement of the Center for Preventive Action

The Center for Preventive Action (CPA) seeks to help prevent, defuse, or resolve deadly conflicts around the world and to expand the body of knowledge on conflict prevention. It does so by creating a forum in which representatives of governments, international organizations, nongovernmental organizations, corporations, and civil society can gather to develop operational and timely strategies for promoting peace in specific conflict situations. The center focuses on conflicts in countries or regions that affect U.S. interests, but may be otherwise overlooked; where prevention appears possible; and when the resources of the Council on Foreign Relations can make a difference. The center does this by

- Issuing Council Special Reports to evaluate and respond rapidly to developing conflict situations and formulate timely, concrete policy recommendations that the U.S. government, international community, and local actors can use to limit the potential for deadly violence.
- Engaging the U.S. government and news media in conflict prevention efforts. CPA staff members meet with administration officials and members of Congress to brief on CPA's findings and recommendations; facilitate contacts between U.S. officials and important local and external actors; and raise awareness among journalists of potential flashpoints around the globe.
- Building networks with international organizations and institutions to complement and leverage the Council's established influence in the U.S. policy arena and increase the impact of CPA's recommendations.
- Providing a source of expertise on conflict prevention to include research, case studies, and lessons learned from past conflicts that policymakers and private citizens can use to prevent or mitigate future deadly conflicts.

Council Special Reports

Published by the Council on Foreign Relations

Countering Criminal Violence in Central America
Michael Shifter; CSR No. 64, April 2012
A Center for Preventive Action Report

Saudi Arabia in the New Middle East
F. Gregory Gause III; CSR No. 63, December 2011
A Center for Preventive Action Report

Partners in Preventive Action: The United States and International Institutions
Paul B. Stares and Micah Zenko; CSR No. 62, September 2011
A Center for Preventive Action Report

Justice Beyond The Hague: Supporting the Prosecution of International Crimes in National Courts
David A. Kaye; CSR No. 61, June 2011

The Drug War in Mexico: Confronting a Shared Threat
David A. Shirk; CSR No. 60, March 2011
A Center for Preventive Action Report

UN Security Council Enlargement and U.S. Interests
Kara C. McDonald and Stewart M. Patrick; CSR No. 59, December 2010
An International Institutions and Global Governance Program Report

Congress and National Security
Kay King; CSR No. 58, November 2010

Toward Deeper Reductions in U.S. and Russian Nuclear Weapons
Micah Zenko; CSR No. 57, November 2010
A Center for Preventive Action Report

Internet Governance in an Age of Cyber Insecurity
Robert K. Knake; CSR No. 56, September 2010
An International Institutions and Global Governance Program Report

From Rome to Kampala: The U.S. Approach to the 2010 International Criminal Court Review Conference
Vijay Padmanabhan; CSR No. 55, April 2010

Strengthening the Nuclear Nonproliferation Regime
Paul Lettow; CSR No. 54, April 2010
An International Institutions and Global Governance Program Report

The Russian Economic Crisis
Jeffrey Mankoff; CSR No. 53, April 2010

Somalia: A New Approach
Bronwyn E. Bruton; CSR No. 52, March 2010
A Center for Preventive Action Report

The Future of NATO
James M. Goldgeier; CSR No. 51, February 2010
An International Institutions and Global Governance Program Report

The United States in the New Asia
Evan A. Feigenbaum and Robert A. Manning; CSR No. 50, November 2009
An International Institutions and Global Governance Program Report

Intervention to Stop Genocide and Mass Atrocities: International Norms and U.S. Policy
Matthew C. Waxman; CSR No. 49, October 2009
An International Institutions and Global Governance Program Report

Enhancing U.S. Preventive Action
Paul B. Stares and Micah Zenko; CSR No. 48, October 2009
A Center for Preventive Action Report

The Canadian Oil Sands: Energy Security vs. Climate Change
Michael A. Levi; CSR No. 47, May 2009
A Maurice R. Greenberg Center for Geoeconomic Studies Report

The National Interest and the Law of the Sea
Scott G. Borgerson; CSR No. 46, May 2009

Lessons of the Financial Crisis
Benn Steil; CSR No. 45, March 2009
A Maurice R. Greenberg Center for Geoeconomic Studies Report

Global Imbalances and the Financial Crisis
Steven Dunaway; CSR No. 44, March 2009
A Maurice R. Greenberg Center for Geoeconomic Studies Report

Eurasian Energy Security
Jeffrey Mankoff; CSR No. 43, February 2009

Preparing for Sudden Change in North Korea
Paul B. Stares and Joel S. Wit; CSR No. 42, January 2009
A Center for Preventive Action Report

Averting Crisis in Ukraine
Steven Pifer; CSR No. 41, January 2009
A Center for Preventive Action Report

Congo: Securing Peace, Sustaining Progress
Anthony W. Gambino; CSR No. 40, October 2008
A Center for Preventive Action Report

Deterring State Sponsorship of Nuclear Terrorism
Michael A. Levi; CSR No. 39, September 2008

China, Space Weapons, and U.S. Security
Bruce W. MacDonald; CSR No. 38, September 2008

Sovereign Wealth and Sovereign Power: The Strategic Consequences of American Indebtedness
Brad W. Setser; CSR No. 37, September 2008
A Maurice R. Greenberg Center for Geoeconomic Studies Report

Securing Pakistan's Tribal Belt
Daniel Markey; CSR No. 36, July 2008 (Web-only release) and August 2008
A Center for Preventive Action Report

Avoiding Transfers to Torture
Ashley S. Deeks; CSR No. 35, June 2008

Global FDI Policy: Correcting a Protectionist Drift
David M. Marchick and Matthew J. Slaughter; CSR No. 34, June 2008
A Maurice R. Greenberg Center for Geoeconomic Studies Report

Dealing with Damascus: Seeking a Greater Return on U.S.-Syria Relations
Mona Yacoubian and Scott Lasensky; CSR No. 33, June 2008
A Center for Preventive Action Report

Climate Change and National Security: An Agenda for Action
Joshua W. Busby; CSR No. 32, November 2007
A Maurice R. Greenberg Center for Geoeconomic Studies Report

Planning for Post-Mugabe Zimbabwe
Michelle D. Gavin; CSR No. 31, October 2007
A Center for Preventive Action Report

The Case for Wage Insurance
Robert J. LaLonde; CSR No. 30, September 2007
A Maurice R. Greenberg Center for Geoeconomic Studies Report

Reform of the International Monetary Fund
Peter B. Kenen; CSR No. 29, May 2007
A Maurice R. Greenberg Center for Geoeconomic Studies Report

Nuclear Energy: Balancing Benefits and Risks
Charles D. Ferguson; CSR No. 28, April 2007

Nigeria: Elections and Continuing Challenges
Robert I. Rotberg; CSR No. 27, April 2007
A Center for Preventive Action Report

The Economic Logic of Illegal Immigration
Gordon H. Hanson; CSR No. 26, April 2007
A Maurice R. Greenberg Center for Geoeconomic Studies Report

The United States and the WTO Dispute Settlement System
Robert Z. Lawrence; CSR No. 25, March 2007
A Maurice R. Greenberg Center for Geoeconomic Studies Report

Bolivia on the Brink
Eduardo A. Gamarra; CSR No. 24, February 2007
A Center for Preventive Action Report

After the Surge: The Case for U.S. Military Disengagement from Iraq
Steven N. Simon; CSR No. 23, February 2007

Darfur and Beyond: What Is Needed to Prevent Mass Atrocities
Lee Feinstein; CSR No. 22, January 2007

Avoiding Conflict in the Horn of Africa: U.S. Policy Toward Ethiopia and Eritrea
Terrence Lyons; CSR No. 21, December 2006
A Center for Preventive Action Report

Living with Hugo: U.S. Policy Toward Hugo Chávez's Venezuela
Richard Lapper; CSR No. 20, November 2006
A Center for Preventive Action Report

Reforming U.S. Patent Policy: Getting the Incentives Right
Keith E. Maskus; CSR No. 19, November 2006
A Maurice R. Greenberg Center for Geoeconomic Studies Report

Foreign Investment and National Security: Getting the Balance Right
Alan P. Larson and David M. Marchick; CSR No. 18, July 2006
A Maurice R. Greenberg Center for Geoeconomic Studies Report

Challenges for a Postelection Mexico: Issues for U.S. Policy
Pamela K. Starr; CSR No. 17, June 2006 (Web-only release) and November 2006

U.S.-India Nuclear Cooperation: A Strategy for Moving Forward
Michael A. Levi and Charles D. Ferguson; CSR No. 16, June 2006

Generating Momentum for a New Era in U.S.-Turkey Relations
Steven A. Cook and Elizabeth Sherwood-Randall; CSR No. 15, June 2006

Peace in Papua: Widening a Window of Opportunity
Blair A. King; CSR No. 14, March 2006
A Center for Preventive Action Report

Neglected Defense: Mobilizing the Private Sector to Support Homeland Security
Stephen E. Flynn and Daniel B. Prieto; CSR No. 13, March 2006

Afghanistan's Uncertain Transition From Turmoil to Normalcy
Barnett R. Rubin; CSR No. 12, March 2006
A Center for Preventive Action Report

Preventing Catastrophic Nuclear Terrorism
Charles D. Ferguson; CSR No. 11, March 2006

Getting Serious About the Twin Deficits
Menzie D. Chinn; CSR No. 10, September 2005
A Maurice R. Greenberg Center for Geoeconomic Studies Report

Both Sides of the Aisle: A Call for Bipartisan Foreign Policy
Nancy E. Roman; CSR No. 9, September 2005

Forgotten Intervention? What the United States Needs to Do in the Western Balkans
Amelia Branczik and William L. Nash; CSR No. 8, June 2005
A Center for Preventive Action Report

A New Beginning: Strategies for a More Fruitful Dialogue with the Muslim World
Craig Charney and Nicole Yakatan; CSR No. 7, May 2005

Power-Sharing in Iraq
David L. Phillips; CSR No. 6, April 2005
A Center for Preventive Action Report

Giving Meaning to "Never Again": Seeking an Effective Response to the Crisis in Darfur and Beyond
Cheryl O. Igiri and Princeton N. Lyman; CSR No. 5, September 2004

Freedom, Prosperity, and Security: The G8 Partnership with Africa: Sea Island 2004 and Beyond
J. Brian Atwood, Robert S. Browne, and Princeton N. Lyman; CSR No. 4, May 2004

Addressing the HIV/AIDS Pandemic: A U.S. Global AIDS Strategy for the Long Term
Daniel M. Fox and Princeton N. Lyman; CSR No. 3, May 2004
Cosponsored with the Milbank Memorial Fund

Challenges for a Post-Election Philippines
Catharin E. Dalpino; CSR No. 2, May 2004
A Center for Preventive Action Report

Stability, Security, and Sovereignty in the Republic of Georgia
David L. Phillips; CSR No. 1, January 2004
A Center for Preventive Action Report

Note: Council Special Reports are available for download from CFR's website, www.cfr.org.
For more information, email publications@cfr.org.